Contents

AaAaAaAaAaAaAaA

Animals in danger!

Thousands of **species**, or types, of animals are in danger of disappearing from Earth forever. When an animal becomes **extinct**, we will never see it again. Many animals are at risk of dying out in the **wild**. The wild is places that are not controlled by people. The chart on the next page explains the words scientists use to describe animals that are in danger of becoming extinct.

Dinosaurs are extinct animals. There are no dinosaurs left on Earth.

AaBbCcDdEeFfGgHh

The ABCs of Endangered Animals

Bobbie Kalman

Crabtree Publishing Company
www.crabtreebooks.com

KkLlMmNnOoPpQqR

The ABCs of the Natural World

Created by Bobbie Kalman

Dedicated by Enlynne Paterson
To the Paterson, Laing, and Pasquale gang, and their animals:
Barney, Muffin, Sassy, Jimmee, Tyson, and Emma

Author and Editor-in-Chief
Bobbie Kalman

Research
Enlynne Paterson

Editor
Kathy Middleton

Proofreader
Crystal Sikkens

Photo research
Bobbie Kalman
Crystal Sikkens

Design
Bobbie Kalman
Katherine Berti
Samantha Crabtree (cover)

Production coordinator
Katherine Berti

Illustrations
Barbara Bedell: pages 1 (gorilla, leopard, komodo dragon, and rhino), 5 (bottom), 19 (numbat)
Katherine Berti: pages 1 (chimp, elephant, manatee, and zebra), 5 (top), 19 (termites), 24 (black sea turtle)
Cori Marvin: pages 1 (bat), 6
Bonna Rouse: pages 1 (bear), 18, 21, 24 (all except black sea turtle), 30
Margaret Amy Salter: page 1 (penguin, butterfly, monkeys, and wolf)
Tiffany Wybouw: page 1 (frog and turtle)

Photographs
© Beste, Rowan/Animals Animals - Earth Scenes: page 19
© Merlin D. Tuttle/Bat Conservation International: page 6
© BigStockPhoto.com: page 11 (right)
© Dreamstime.com: pages 12, 13 (top), 28 (top)
© Greg Koch, gkphotography.net: page 29
© iStockphoto.com: pages 8 (top), 30 (left)
© Charlie Hamilton James/naturepl.com: page 28 (bottom)
© Photos.com: page 5
© Doug Perrine/SeaPics.com: page 18
© Shutterstock.com: pages 1, 3, 4, 7, 8 (bottom), 9, 10 (right), 13 (bottom), 14, 15, 16, 17, 20, 21, 22, 23, 24, 25, 26, 27, 30 (right), 31
© Wikipedia: Dave Pape: page 10 (left)
Other images by Digital Vision

Library and Archives Canada Cataloguing in Publication

Kalman, Bobbie, 1947-
        The ABCs of endangered animals / Bobbie Kalman.

(The ABCs of the natural world)
Includes index.
ISBN 978-0-7787-3415-4 (bound).--ISBN 978-0-7787-3435-2 (pbk.)

        1. Rare animals--Juvenile literature. 2. Endangered species--Juvenile literature. 3. English language--Alphabet--Juvenile literature. I. Title. II. Series: Kalman, Bobbie, 1947- . ABCs of the natural world.

QL83.K34 2009   j591.68   C2008-907904-3

Library of Congress Cataloging-in-Publication Data

Kalman, Bobbie.
  The ABCs of endangered animals / Bobbie Kalman.
        p. cm. -- (The ABCs of the natural world)
  Includes index.
  ISBN 978-0-7787-3435-2 (pbk. : alk. paper) -- ISBN 978-0-7787-3415-4 (reinforced library binding : alk. paper)
  1. Endangered species--Juvenile literature. 2. English language--Alphabet--Juvenile literature. 3. Alphabet books. I. Title. II. Series.

QL83.K36 2009
591.68--dc22

2008052412

Crabtree Publishing Company
www.crabtreebooks.com   1-800-387-7650

Published in Canada
Crabtree Publishing
616 Welland Ave.
St. Catharines, Ontario
L2M 5V6

Published in the United States
Crabtree Publishing
PMB16A
350 Fifth Ave., Suite 3308
New York, NY 10118

Published in the United Kingdom
Crabtree Publishing
White Cross Mills
High Town, Lancaster
LA1 4XS

Published in Australia
Crabtree Publishing
386 Mt. Alexander Rd.
Ascot Vale (Melbourne)
VIC 3032

A is for apes

Chimpanzees, gorillas, and orangutans are **apes**. Many kinds of apes are endangered. The main threat to apes and most other animals on Earth is that they are losing their homes in the wild.

chimpanzee

orangutan mother and baby

Words to know

Scientists use these words to describe animals in the wild that are in danger.

vulnerable Describes animals that may become endangered because they are facing certain risks

endangered Describes animals that are in danger of dying out in the wild

critically endangered Describes animals that are at high risk of dying out in the wild

extinct Describes animals that have died out or animals that have not been seen in the wild for at least 50 years

gorilla

B b B b B b B b B b B b B b B

Big bats, small bats

Bats are the only **mammals** that can fly. Mammals are animals with hair or fur. Mammal mothers can feed their babies milk from their bodies. Some bats are big, and some are small. Big bats are called **megabats**. Small bats are called **microbats**. About one-quarter of the bats on Earth are endangered. Many bats are dying from harmful chemicals in the air and water.

This endangered bat is a Mexican long-nosed bat. It lives in Mexico and in Texas. The Mexican long-nosed bat is endangered because it cannot find enough food to eat.

6

C c C c C c C c C c C c C c C c

Chimpanzees

Chimpanzees live on **savannas**, or grasslands, and in rain forests. Many rain forests are being cut down, leaving chimps with nowhere to live.

Once there were millions of chimps, or chimpanzees. Now, chimpanzees are endangered and could become extinct within 50 years. Chimps are being hunted for their meat. Many babies are also being trapped to be sold as pets. **Poachers** often kill mothers that try to protect the babies from being taken.

Chimps can walk on their back legs for short distances.

Dancing lemurs

Lemurs are found on Madagascar, an **island** near Africa. Islands are areas of land with water all around them. There are many kinds of lemurs. Verreaux's sifaka is known as the "dancing lemur." Sifakas live mainly in trees, but when they are on the ground, they move as if they are dancing. Sifakas are **herbivores**. Herbivores eat plant foods such as leaves, flowers, and fruit.

Most lemurs are endangered or vulnerable because their forest homes are being cut down.

Endangered elephants

Elephants are the largest land animals on earth. They live in Asia and Africa. Both male and female African elephants have tusks, but only male Asian elephants have them. Both kinds of elephants are endangered. They need a lot of food, but food is now hard to find!

Asian elephants have small ears. Many Asian elephants live with people.

*Some people put electric fences around their farms to stop elephants from eating their **crops**. The fences shock animals that go near them. This elephant baby has walked under an electric fence, but its mother is too tall to get through. What might happen to the baby?*

These elephants are African elephants. African elephants have tusks and big ears.

9

F f F f F f F f F f F f F f F f F f

Fantastic frogs

Frogs live in all kinds of habitats, except in very cold areas. Most live near water. Frogs are very sensitive to changes in their **habitats**. Habitats are the natural homes of animals. People are draining the water from the swamps and ponds where frogs live. **Global warming** is also causing problems for frogs. Global warming is the steady rise in Earth's temperature. It causes harmful **fungi** to grow on the skin of frogs. The fungi make it difficult for frogs to breathe.

The Panamanian golden frog may be extinct in the wild. No one has seen one in its habitat since 2006. A few are still alive in zoos. These frogs died because their skin was covered by fungi.

Poison dart frogs

Poison dart frogs have brightly colored bodies and live in rain forests. All these frogs have poison in their skin, which makes them taste terrible to **predators**. Predators are animals that hunt and eat other animals. Many species of poison dart frogs are critically endangered. The blue poison dart frog below is vulnerable.

G g G g G g G g G g G g G g G g G g

Great gorillas

Mountain gorillas are critically endangered. They are almost extinct in the wild. Mountain gorillas are **great apes**. Great apes are the largest **primates**. Primates are very intelligent animals. People are primates, too. Poverty and wars in Africa are making it hard for people to find or afford food. Mountain gorillas are being hunted because their meat is cheap and easy to get. Another threat to many gorillas is the loss of their habitats, where the animals find food. Mountain gorillas eat mainly plants.

Gorillas live in family groups of five to ten gorillas. Mother gorillas take good care of their babies.

Habitat loss

Each year, there are more people on Earth. That means they need more food and homes. To grow more food and build more homes, people are taking over animal habitats, leaving animals with nowhere to live. Losing homes is called **habitat loss**. When animals cannot find food and new homes, they die. Most animals become endangered due to habitat loss.

These animals are endangered wild dogs called dholes. Dholes live in Asia. They live in forests, grasslands, and on mountains. They are losing their homes in all of these habitats, however, because people are building more farms and cities. Dholes are sometimes hunted because they eat farm animals. They are also run over by cars on roads that have been built through their habitats.

Polar bears are losing their habitat because of global warming. Global warming is causing more sea ice to melt, especially near the North and South poles. Polar bears live near the North Pole. They hunt seals in the ocean, drag them onto ice, and eat them there. The melting of the polar bear's sea-ice habitat is taking away the polar bear's way of hunting food. It is forcing polar bears to find food on land. Some bears are starving because there is not enough food for them to eat.

polar bears eating seal

swan covered in oil

This was once a beautiful mountain lake. Now it looks like a garbage dump. When people **pollute**, or dirty, land and water, they make the animals that live there sick and cause them to die.

Insects in trouble

This bee was covered in pollen when it visited a flower to drink some nectar.

Some people collect beautiful butterflies and sell them. Unfortunately, many butterfly collectors trap and kill butterflies that are endangered.

Insects are small animals with six legs. Some insects also have wings. Most people do not know that insects are endangered, but many insects are dying off.

Helpful insects

Some insects eat **nectar** and **pollen**. Nectar is a liquid, and pollen is a powder. Both are found in flowers. When insects such as butterflies or bees look for nectar and pollen, some of the pollen sticks to their bodies. They carry the pollen to other plants. Plants need pollen from other plants to make new plants. In the past few years, however, many bees have died. Scientists feel that **pesticides** may be the main cause. Insects also die because people cut down too many plants, and there is not enough food for insects to eat.

Japanese cranes

The Japanese crane is also called the red-crowned crane. This large crane has a patch of red skin on its head, which becomes bright red when the crane gets angry or excited. Japanese cranes are known for their beautiful **courtship dances**. Some Japanese cranes live in Siberia in the spring and summer and then **migrate** to Japan, Korea, and China in the fall. The other group lives in Japan all year long. The Japanese crane was almost extinct in the 1920s, but now there are about 2,500 of these birds in the wild.

*In East Asia, the red-crowned crane is a **symbol** of peace, happiness, and a long life.*

15

Kk Kk Kk Kk Kk Kk Kk Kk

Komodo dragons

*Komodo dragons are **cold-blooded** animals. Cold-blooded animals cannot make heat inside their bodies. Some **bask**, or lie in the sun, to warm themselves. This Komodo dragon is lying on a warm rock. The rock is heating its belly while the sun warms its back.*

Komodo dragons are the largest lizards in the world. They are named after Komodo Island, one of the four small islands on which they live. Komodo dragons eat mainly deer, but they also hunt wild pigs, birds, and other animals. There are only 3,000 to 5,000 Komodo dragons left on Earth. Komodos are vulnearable because people are taking more of their habitat, and there are fewer deer for them to eat. Many are starving.

A Komodo dragon hunts by flicking out its tongue. Its tongue takes the smell from the air and pushes it against the roof of the mouth. The Komodo dragon can then "taste" the animal's smell.

Lovely leopards

*Leopards are predators. They hunt and eat other animals, such as deer, monkeys, big birds, and snakes. They often drag their **prey** high up into trees, to keep other predators from stealing it. Prey is an animal that a predator hunts.*

Leopards live in Asia and Africa. They are wild cats with beautiful spotted fur. There are eight species of leopards. All leopards are endangered. People have built towns, roads, and farms on leopard habitats. Farmers often kill leopards to protect their farm animals. Leopards are also being hunted for their fur, bones, whiskers, and meat.

Leopard preserves

To help protect leopards, many countries have turned leopard habitats into **preserves**. Preserves are large areas of land where leopards are protected by **rangers**. Rangers are people who keep animals safe and help the ones that get sick or hurt.

It is easy to see the spots of the baby leopard above, but the spots of black leopards are much harder to spot.

M m M m M m M m M m M

Manatee mammals

Manatees are **marine mammals**. Marine mammals live and find food mainly in oceans. Manatees live in warm, shallow waters. They live under water, but they must swim to the surface to breathe air—even while they are sleeping. There are three species of manatees—Amazonian manatees, West African manatees, and West Indian manatees. All manatees are endangered. Many are killed by boats or get caught in fishing nets. Some are poisoned by chemicals in oceans.

The Florida manatee is a type of West Indian manatee. It swims in oceans around Florida.
This manatee calf is drinking its mother's milk.

Nn Nn Nn Nn Nn Nn Nn Nn

Numbats

Numbats are gentle, slow-moving animals that live in Western Australia. They are mammals called **marsupials**. Most marsupials have pouches in which they carry their babies, but numbats do not have pouches. Their babies cling to the belly fur of their mothers while they grow. Numbats use their long, sticky tongues to catch and eat termites. They can eat thousands of termites a day! Numbats are endangered. Their habitat is being destroyed to build farms and homes. Many numbats are also eaten by foxes, wild cats, and dogs.

Numbats eat termites.

termites

Numbats are about the size of squirrels.

Orange orangutans

Orangutans are apes with orange-colored hair and very long arms. They live in **jungles**. Jungles are hot forests with many trees. Orangutans eat, play, and sleep in the trees. They use branches and leaves to build nests. Orangutans are endangered because of habitat loss. They are also being caught and sold **illegally** as pets.

Orangutans have lost most of their forest habitat to logging. These apes once lived all over Southeast Asia, but now they can be found only on the islands of Borneo and Sumatra. The Borneo orangutans are endangered, and the Sumatran orangutans are critically endangered.

Pet traders killed the mother of this orangutan baby. The baby is now very sick. Many baby animals cannot survive without their mothers. This baby has been rescued by a ranger.

p P p P p P p P p P p P p P p P p P
Pandas on preserves

The giant panda is a well-known endangered animal. Its picture reminds people to help all endangered animals. The giant panda is a large, strong bear that is also gentle and shy.

Bamboo eaters

Pandas eat only bamboo, but many bamboo forests are being cut down. Most pandas live on preserves, where food is easy to find. Preserves also protect pandas from poachers, who want panda fur.

Panda cubs stay with their mothers until they are two years old. Female pandas have very few cubs.

Pandas eat a lot of bamboo in one day!

Pandas are good climbers, even as babies. They often climb trees to take long naps.

Q q Q q Q q Q q Q q Q q Q q

Quolls or "native cats"

Quolls live in Australia, Tasmania, and Papua, New Guinea. They used to live all over Australia, but most of their habitats have been taken over by people or destroyed by fire. Many quolls are also being eaten by predators such as foxes and pet cats. Quolls feed on birds, insects, reptiles, and small mammals.

Quolls are active at night and sleep during the day. This quoll lives in a tree log.

Quolls are called "native cats." Some are the size of cats.

RrRrRrRrRrRrRrRr
Rhinoceros in trouble

The rhinoceros, or rhino, is the second-largest land animal, after the elephant. There are five species of rhinos. Black rhinos and white rhinos live in Africa. Javan, Sumatran, and Indian rhinos live in Asia. The black, white, and Sumatran rhinos have two horns. The Indian and Javan rhinos have one horn. The Javan, Sumatran, and black rhinos are critically endangered. There are fewer than 60 Javan rhinoceros alive in the world. They are the most endangered large mammals on Earth!

black rhinoceros

Poachers hunt rhinos for their horns.

white rhinoceros

Indian rhinoceros

This Javan rhino and its calf are in a zoo. Javan rhinos are the most endangered rhinos.

The Sumatran rhino is the smallest rhino. It is critically endangered.

Sea turtles

Sea turtles are marine reptiles. They live in oceans and swim to the surface to breathe air. There are eight species of sea turtles. All are endangered, but the hawksbill, Kemp's ridley, and leatherback are critically endangered. Sea turtles are killed for their meat and beautiful shells. Many are also caught in fishing nets or get tangled in garbage. Sea turtles lay their eggs on beaches, but hotels and homes are taking up more room on many beaches.

The loggerhead has a very large head.

The flatback has a flat shell.

The olive ridley is a small sea turtle.

The hawksbill's jaw looks like a hawk's beak.

Green sea turtles are killed for their meat and fat.

Black sea turtles are related to green sea turtles.

The leatherback is the largest sea turtle

The Kemp's ridley is the smallest sea turtle.

Tt Tt Tt Tt Tt Tt Tt Tt Tt Tt Tt Tt

Tiger, tiger

Tigers are wild cats. They are the biggest cats. Tigers are predators that hunt other animals for food. Tigers like to live near trees and water. They are good swimmers. Some live in steamy hot jungles, and others live in snowy mountain forests.

The Siberian, or Amur tiger, is the biggest tiger. It is also critically endangered.

Endangered cats

Tigers are endangered because people are cutting down forests and polluting the land and water where tigers live. Tigers are also hunted for their fur and body parts. Tiger whiskers and bones are used to make medicines. Fewer tiger cubs are being born, and the tiger population is getting smaller every year.

The Sumatran tiger is the smallest tiger. It is critically endangered.

Uakari monkeys

The tails of red uakaris are shorter than the tails of other monkeys.

Uakaris are monkeys. This uakari is called a bald uakari because it has very little fur on its face or head. It is also known as a red uakari because of its red face. Uakaris with bright red faces are healthier than those with pale pink faces.

Amazon monkeys

Uakaris live in the Amazon rain forest in Brazil and Peru. During the day, uakaris look for leaves, fruits, seeds, and insects to eat in the branches of trees. At night, they sleep high in the treetops.

Living in groups

Red uakaris live in groups of up to 100 monkeys. They are threatened by habitat loss and are also hunted for meat.

Vietnam monkeys

Vietnam is a country in Southeast Asia. It shares borders with Laos, China, and Cambodia. It is the home of monkeys called douc langurs. The douc langurs shown here are called red-shanked douc langurs because their **shanks**, or legs, are red.

Forest habitats

Douc langurs live in different kinds of forests. They eat fruits, leaves, seeds, and flowers. These monkeys are endangered because many forests are being cut down in Vietnam. They are also hunted for their meat, bones, and other body parts, which are used to make medicines.

Wild wolves

This mother and her pups are gray wolves.

Wolves are the largest of the dog family, which also includes coyotes, jackals, foxes, and pet dogs. There are three kinds of wolves—gray wolves, Ethiopian wolves, and red wolves. Wolves live in **packs,** or groups, of four to seven family members. A pack works as a team to hunt large prey, such as deer and moose.

Most endangered

Some kinds of gray wolves are vulnerable, and some are endangered. Ethiopian wolves are critically endangered. There are fewer than 550 of them left on Earth. Red wolves are also critically endangered.

These wolves are Ethiopian wolves. Wolf mothers have between one and seven pups at a time.

Red wolves

Thirty years ago, red wolves were extinct in the wild, but a few of them were being raised in **captivity**. The wolves were then released into the wild places where red wolves once lived. Now there are about 300 red wolves, but only 100 of them live in the wild.

Xerces Society

The Xerces Society is a conservation group dedicated to protecting **invertebrates**. Invertebrates are animals without backbones. Most invertebrates are insects such as butterflies, bees, and beetles. This conservation group is named after the Xerces butterfly, which is now extinct. The Xerces Society teaches people how to save invertebrates and their habitats.

You can help!

You can help animals by caring for their habitats. You can pick up garbage and litter and ask your parents to stop using pesticides. Watch animals in your area to see how they live. Learn as much as you can about endangered animals and tell other people about them. Join a nature club and raise money to help endangered animals. Reduce, reuse, and recycle. It helps animals and you!

Go green!

Ask your parents to help you build a bat house. You can find directions at www.batcon.org

30

zZzZzZzZzZzZzZzZzZzZ

Zebras in the wild

Zebras are wild horses with stripes. The three main groups of zebras are plains zebras, mountain zebras, and Grévy's zebras. Grévy's zebras are endangered. They are the largest zebras and are more like horses than like zebras. All zebras are losing their grazing areas to people and farm animals. Farm animals graze in zebra habitats, leaving zebras with fewer places to find food and water.

Many endangered zebras live on preserves.

Grévy's zebras are the largest and heaviest zebras. Their stripes are narrower than the stripes of other zebras.

People still hunt zebras for their beautiful striped skins, which are often used for making rugs.

A a B b C c D d E e F f G g H

Glossary

Note: Some boldfaced words are defined where they appear in the book.

ape A kind of primate that can walk almost upright and has no tail

captivity A state of being in an enclosed area such as a zoo

crops Plants grown by people for food

courtship dance A movement made by an animal to attract a mate

extinct Describing a plant or an animal that is no longer found on Earth

fungi A group of living things, such as yeasts, molds, and mushrooms

illegally Carrying out an act that is against the law

mammal An animal with hair or fur that drinks its mother's milk

migrate To move from one location to another in order to mate, find food, or enjoy better weather

pesticide A chemical used to kill insects

poacher A person who hunts animals where it is against the law to do so

pollute To add harmful waste, making an area unfit for living things

primate A mammal with a very large brain that can climb trees

species A group of closely related living things that can have babies

symbol Something that stands for something else

Index

Printed in the U.S.A. - CG